Apostle of Her Culture

Compiled by Christopher Davis

Copyright © 2020 Christopher Davis

All rights reserved. No part of this book may be reproduced, scanned, or distributed in any printed or electronic form or by any means without prior written consent of the publisher, except for brief quotes used in reviews.

Please do not participate in or encourage piracy of copyrighted materials in violation of the author's rights. Purchase only authorized editions.

Published by

Hadassah's Crown Publishing, LLC

Simpsonville, SC 29681

Library of Congress Control Number: 2020915182

ISBN 9781950894246

Printed in the United States of America

Dedication

This book is dedicated to the memory of the following: Mr. Richard Askins, Sr. & Mrs. Martha Davis-Askins, Mr. James Dewitt & Mrs. Ethel Dewitt, Bishop R.F. Davis & Mother Iola B. Davis, Bishop Spencer Davis, Rev. Dr. Henry McGill, Rev. Truman C. Tart, Rev. H.K. Phillips, Rev. Dr. John Duncan (AKA Michael Fogan), Dr. Mary G. Eaddy, Dr. David Dorsey, Mr. Samuel Rowell, Sr., Ms. Virginia Rowell, Mrs. Betty Jo McCall, Ms. Valerie Rowe-Jackson, Mrs. Mae Vern Hendley, Mrs. Henrietta Platt, Dr. Debra Crawford, Mrs. Annie Belle Bellinger-Crawford, Mrs. Teressa E. Stoudemire, Ms. Debra Dorsey Fling, Mrs. Geneva Hall-McNeil, Mrs. Alice Davis-Owens, Mrs. Essie Terry Davis-Shepherd, Mrs. Doshia Louise Davis-Wilson, Mrs. Mary Davis-McLeod, Ms. Ella Davis, Ms. Olena Davis, Mrs. Donna Thomas, Mrs. Constance Smith, Elder Gregory Davis, Mrs. Fran C. Fields and Mrs. Audrey Johnson-Thornton.

This book is also dedicated in honor of a few extra special persons who over the years have worked in so many capacities to make certain that the first edition of this series comes to fruition. My mother, Ms. Dorothy J. Davis, Mother Josephine West, Mr. John Washington & Mrs. Michele Dickerson-Washington, Rev. Cecil L. Bromell & Mrs. Poiette McGill-Bromell, Mrs. Jacqueline Jackson-McGill, Mrs. Jacqueline Baker-Hall, Ms. Gwendolyn Hall, Rev. Virgil Hammett, Mrs. Jeanette H. Scott, Dr. Matrell Eaddy-Sturkey, Professor Barbara S. Code, Mrs. Luevenia Shipman-Wright, Rev. Kenneth C. Taylor, Dr. Walter James, Sr. (Uncle Big Bubba), Ms. Lisa Seabrook, Mrs. Lillian Jones-Wilson, Rev. Glen Shepherd, Mrs. Nadine Harris-Foxworth, Mr. Jermaine Tart, Deacon Isaac Black & Mrs. Nicole Black, Dr. A.C. Robinson, Dr. Ralph Canty, Dr. Jacqueline Wright-Canty, Past Grand Master Lewis Nelson, Rev. Richard W. Crummy & Mrs. Bonnie Crummy, Mrs. Angela Smith-Frazier, Rev. Henry Peoples & Mrs. Beatrice Peoples, Mrs. Fran Fields, Mrs. Charlie Mae Gunn, Mrs. Patricia Ann Thomas, Dr. Barbara Rhodes (SUNYIT New York), Mrs. Lillian Barnett, Mrs. Alice C. Tisdale (Former First Lady of Claflin University, Orangeburg, South Carolina), Mrs. Harriett Williams, Ms. Jacqueline D. Crawford, Ms. Wood Ann Ellis, Mrs. Bertha M. Drake, Mrs. Sallie McDaniel-Davis, Ms. Mattie H. Israel, Ms. Alice M. Williamson, Mrs. Brenda Thompson-Jamerson, Mrs. Rachelle Jamerson-Holmes, Mrs. Sylvia Rogers, Rev. Curtis Campbell, Rev. Frederick Johnson, Rev. Oliver Davis, Jr., Dr. Mack T. Hines, Former State Representative Joe Brown, Former Senator Maggie Wallace-Glover, Mr. Berry, Mr.

Lynwood McDaniel, Mr. John Evans Mr. Arthur Evans Jr. & Sr., Mr. Gerald Evans, Ms. Annette Evans and Mrs. Yolonda Brown-Davis.

A special dedication to all of my siblings; in particular; Mr. Christopher D. Moody, Mr. David L. Rowell (AKA Dave) and Mrs. Jacqueline Rowell-Mason. My nieces featured on the cover, Shariya Moody and Kayla McGirt. All of the parishioners of the Greater Highway Churches of Christ International, Church of God in Christ International, Bethlehem Missionary Baptist Church; Bethel AME Church, Britton's Neck, SC; St. John AME Church, Turner Memorial AME Church, Turner Monumental AME Church, Greater Singletary AME Church, St. John AME Church, Mill Creek Missionary Baptist Church and Mt. Zion AME Sellers to name a few. Photo credits: Cover Mr. Orlando Davis-Orangeburg, SC, Christopher Davis and Mr. William Wade, Philadelphia, Pennsylvania. Typing Credit: Marion High School Typing Class: Tamea Crawford, Aniyiah Eaddy, Ny'Kera Green, Jasmine Harps, Camorie Lewis, Mykala Page, Jakobe Sims, Keionna Steele. Cover graphics: Mr. Charles Spady, Spady Graphics Atlanta, GA.

Purpose

"Every child deserves a champion: an adult who will never give up on them, who understands the power of connection and insists they become the best they can possibly be." Rita Pierson

There were many days I sat in my graduate studies class reading and processing information as it pertained to children and families, and how significant this information was to the Afrocentric perspective used as a model for social work and psychology. There were many days I sat and watched Rita Pierson on *Ted Talks*, absorbing the messages she was conveying.

There were many days I sat and listened to Bishop T.D. Jakes' "Feeding the Dream." Often, I pondered how I could use my artistic abilities to help change the trajectories of the lives of young black boys who may not have the opportunity or opportunities that I had in life to do something creative. There were days when I just sat in class at Clark-Atlanta University and looked out the window to view the skyline of Atlanta. I also stared out of the window while enrolled at Allen University in Columbia, SC, while the thoughts of young people who were not so privileged entered my mind and planted a small picture.

There were days when I had conversations with professors about my aspirations to find out that a number of them could care less. A number of workshops and panel presentations I sat through, whether at Clark-Atlanta, Morehouse, Spelman, or ITC, no matter how many art shows I attended or talked about the power of being self-sufficient and the dream of having an impact on the life of someone less fortunate, I always found professors and panel presenters turned a deaf ear, some not many minutes after they came down off of the platform. There were times I encountered one of the platform presenters or professors from the Atlanta University Center in the Atlanta community, sharing that same conversation, but there was no action. I learned to chalk it up just as it was, "air."

Nonetheless, there were a few professors who encouraged me to stay the course. Whether it was on the campus of Morehouse, Clark-Atlanta, Spelman or Morris Brown, I could visit the offices of these professors and have a conversation, leaving uplifted and encouraged. For the most part, these were professors who didn't spend a great deal of time talking, but they were about the business of the students. They had a genuine concern for the community. One thing I knew for sure though was that I could reach back to my undergraduate professors and converse with them, even one former staff member, Ms. Brenda Chambers, who encouraged me on a regular to go beyond measure, always give a task better than your best shot. Professor Barbara S. Code, who along with Dr. Maxwell Boafo, confirmed that there were no boundaries in terms of the life I sought, there was a universe with no walls, no entrance and no exit, and they always encouraged me to simply go for it.

After thinking over my undergraduate situations and accomplishments, I still pondered over my next move, while I had begun to line things up. I just wasn't sure when to start or where. Day after day, I sat in Atlanta and thought about Philadelphia, a place where I was confident that if I returned there to live, it would be smooth sailing because I had major connections there. But then, that was my comfort zone. I would go from day to day thinking about the speech Dr. Dennis Kimbro delivered during my undergraduate commencement "Let Them Hear You." All of these thoughts and ideas crowded my mind, but I kept moving forward, and remained focused academically.

I always seized opportunities to steal away and listen to Les Brown, Bishop T.D. Jakes, Oprah Winfrey, and when I could Bishop Michael Blue, my former high school English teacher, as my own way of meditating. But one day when I sat and listened to Oprah as she delivered the commencement speech at Spelman College in 2012 via YouTube, the light brightened as she shared three points. It was then that I knew that what I was already doing was shifting the paradigms of what helped me garner success to service and work to bring significance. After hearing Ms. Winfrey break it down, I knew I was on the right path.

From there, I slacked up on sharing my dreams and my visions with professors and various personalities from the AU Center, church members, as well as those who just did not share an interest in what I was doing. Those professors who listened and offered feedback when the lights were dim, and those church members who made purchases or paved the way for purchases, simply realized that my cup was running over. As Ms. Winfrey stated, you cannot spend your life, with your gallon-size offerings, offering them to pint-size people.

One day a friend pointed out the message by Bishop T.D. Jakes about the analogy comparing where giraffes eat from and where turtles eat from. "We eat on the level of our vision," said. Bishop T.D. Jakes. So, I simply stopped sharing with naysayers and moved forward into the realm of service. I thought more and more if I could just have an opportunity to talk to my dad, he would say something that would inspire me to continue on. Unfortunately, he was murdered. But I can never think of a time when he told me that I could not be successful, no matter what the venture I embarked upon.

I began to fine tune all of the notes that I had written all over everywhere and compiling them together. From there I sought to establish an organization comprised of Black women who could relate to my vision, those who wanted to see other young black boys rise to the realm of success through service.

Black boys who could reach back and pull others up and offer them opportunities and platforms to showcase their artistic abilities were sought. Today, we are four years old as an organization named "New Life Hat Society Inc.," which is a vessel of service to myself, my family and my community, as shared by Ms. Winfrey. Knowing that I have stayed the course of making the vision that I often wrote about plain, a vision of empowering black men and boys into the fold of entrepreneurship based upon their artistic abilities, is gratifying, to say the least.

One thing is for certain, I will never take for granted that I was indeed fortunate, because every black boy who possesses an artistic talent doesn't have a family member, or family friend who is a part of an organization like the Links Inc., Girlfriends Inc., sororities like Delta Sigma Theta, Zeta Phi Beta, Alpha Kappa Alpha, or Sigma Gamma Rho. Not every black boy has a connection to organizations like the Order of the Eastern Star, or a Grand Master in a Society of Free and Accepted Masons, organization such as Top Ladies of Distinction, a chain of pastor's wives and pastors alike, male and female who have connections on local, regional and national levels that can enable their success, and so again I don't take that for granted. I also thought about how impactful those connections could be for some other young black boys, and so here we are, after sowing seeds for at least ten years, the first edition of a series of books that deal with historic perspectives of black women who wear hats to church, and an organization on the rise to international recognition.

When you purchase this book or any product sold by this organization, you help make life chances greater for a Black boy in particular, but at the same time for Black and Hispanic youth or a young person of any nationality. Your purchase enables New Life Hat Society to continue to place books written by black authors into their hands, as well as continue to teach them entrepreneurship from a guided curriculum, hone their visual arts skills and provide them with

cultural workshops, counseling services and activities. This organization is able to strengthen these young males culturally, emotionally, intellectually, and impact their lives economically.
Website: newlifehatsociety.org   Email: newlifehatsociety@gmail.com

 Reach out to us as we travel the nation building this organization and improving the lives of young people, creating entrepreneurs, planting seeds of self-sufficiency, developing skilled leaders through reading, based upon their artistic abilities. We have various aspects of fashion and hat shows that we use as a means of generating funds to provide such programs and activities. Call upon us for our shows to include men in stylish hats. We will also provide a speaker for your luncheon through collaborations with our organization.

Who Are These Apostles of Her Culture?

When your children shall ask you in the days to come, "Who are these Apostles of Her Culture or Who is this Woman? What is the significance of this exhibit? What has become of the fabric of these Crown-Bearing Apostles? What then shall you tell them?"

These are they who have been drenched in the political fabric and social engagements of wearing hats to church as black women, which is now being documented in history for the purpose of moving from the realm of oral traditions. How then shall you know her story if you don't know her history? Here you have an interpretation of how these women feel and their own historic landmarks. Here is where you learn the significance of how feminism, professionalization, guilded-age culture, progressivism, public service, the arts and reform merge with fashion. These Apostles created "Couture" in the black community, without even realizing what they were doing. These are they who were simply tired of the drab uniform look from day to day.

"Greetings!" As so eloquently stated originally by Nana Yaa Brayie- in her Libation, we greet and honor these "Queens" adorned in their royal headgear…(slightly tweaked for the purpose of this project.) "Grandpa, what makes the lightning bugs light up?" the little boy asked his grandfather as they walked the country road home one night. With wide-eyed wonder, the child was noticing the fireflies switch their tail lights on and off in the pitch-black darkness. Searching his brain for the profoundly wise, unquestionable answer a little boy needed to hear from his elder and not finding it, Grandpa, hating to admit it, finally answered, "Aye Lord, boy. I don't rightly know. I guess it's just the stuff that's in 'em." As we look around us during times like National Women's History Month, and as we consider the miraculous power of women and we note how women, like the lightning bug, mysteriously light up the darkness wherever they go, we know it is in Divine Order that we offer this sacred ritual to the Divine Feminine energy within all humankind.

We first pour this libation to the Divine Mother of Creation and to all our cosmic mothers, especially to Grandmother Moon, who is now blessing us with her splendid fullness. Then we pour to the extraordinary intelligence and creativity of Earth's first human mothers, African women, the co-founders of all systems of knowledge that civilized the world.

To our enslaved ancestral mothers, who suffered the atrocities of our Maafa (the African Holocaust), and still mustered up enough faith to plan for the unforeseeable, to live through the unthinkable, and to forgive the unforgiveable, all the while maintaining their dignity and self-respect. To the resourcefulness of those mothers who kept us alive against the odds, who, for example, when captured, had the foresight and ingenuity to hide okra seeds and others in their coarse, braided hair so there would be food when they reached whatever place the huge ships were taking them. And, while on the plantations, to encrypt details of escape into the quilt designs they were forced to sew, wash, and hang on clothes lines to dry.

To the fleet-footed bravery of indigenous Native American women, and to the compassion of daring European women who assisted the Africans in this fierce fight for freedom. To the irrepressible spirit of those women who opened the first doors of justice for women such as these, by actively resisting and toppling the "White Only" signs, and to those who just flat out ignored the "Only Men Need Apply" signs of sexist exclusion.

To the determination and creative genius of those women who continue to work miracles in education, religion, the arts and sciences, entertainment, athletics, economics, and more. To the unmitigated courage of women of all ethnic and cultural backgrounds, who in the past, and into modern times, continue to speak out and rise up against the oppressive and suppressive insults and physical assaults so often condoned in patriarchal societies.

To the fearless, fair-minded men whose masculine and feminine aspects are so balanced that they stand with women such as these, on the Laws of Maat, realizing that by honoring all women, they honor the Divine Feminine Principle in themselves. Lastly, no doubt by now, you're thinking of women (historical and/or current figures, including your personal sheroes) whose actual photos you feel belong on this cornerstone "It's just the stuff that's in 'em" list. Take a few moments to prepare to read the historic perspectives as they pertain to their relationships to wearing hats to church and for occasions, and view this portrait showcase.

As you have seen depicted in many films, as well as written by Elizabeth Clark Lewis in *Living In, Living Out*, what else did they know other than wanting to look good for Sunday morning worship? As mentioned earlier, after a week of wearing boring uniforms and some fifty of them with the same look all day every day, these ladies wanted to look and feel different. So they put their best. This enabled onlookers to see feathers, bows, ribbons, buttons, flowers, tall hats, short hats, wide hats, and even the widest hats. Of course, you know they pulled out the "good suit," with the gloves, the handbags and the pumps.

According to one journalist, wearing hats to church carries a strong legacy, so much that it has left an impact upon generations of young girls who grew up into tradition-bearing young ladies. These ladies have often been found associated with organizations and congregations that embrace finer womanhood. Although hat wearing seems to be a little less popular among present generations, some young ladies still manage to find means and ways of continuing the tradition in the form of brunch, big hats and sundresses, with a little mimosa, or getting a hat for the annual Kentucky Derby Theme Parties, and maybe even attending the actual Kentucky Derby itself. Among the most upscale of the theme parties are those hosted by the Links Inc. of Greenville, South Carolina, the Alpha Phi Alpha, and Kappa Alpha Psi Fraternities of Greater Atlanta, Georgia. Here you can find the ladies adorned in some of the most ostentatious, vibrant, colorful and tasteful hats that can be found, accented with apparel that adds spice to what they are cooking up. The aftermath is breathtaking, and causes you to think you are walking into a den of "hats" preparing for battle.

According to Evelyn Higginbotham and other ladies who have adorned their heads with hats, the church is the heart of the Sunday celebration. Historically, it has been the center of political, social, economic, religious and educational affairs. The African American church was not only spiritually important, but also culturally unifying. It was indeed the heart of the African American community. Mrs. Higginbotham specifically stated that the public discourse of the church leaders and members, both male and female, had historically linked social regeneration, in the specific form of racial advancement, to spiritual regeneration.

The church fought against the social injustices that African Americans faced in America. It was also a sanctuary of comfort, where everyone could express themselves freely and unite culturally in their beliefs and life practices. It has been a place to observe, participate in, and experience the reality of owning and directing an institution free from Whites. The church was also an arena where interest groups could articulate and defended their positions collectively. For all these reasons and a host of others, the Black church has served as the organizational hub of Black life.

Black women play an influential role in the church community. They help establish a fine rapport between the minister and congregation. Women of the church run many of the social functions of the church. They rejected a model of womanhood that was fragile and passive, just as they deplored a type pre-occupied with fashion, gossip, and of self-indulgence. They argued that women held the key to social transformation, and thus, America offered them a vast mission field in which to solicit as never before the active participation of self-disciplined, self-sacrificing workers.

Through the convention movement and Nannie Helen Burroughs, African American women would be viewed as leaders of their churches and communities. In 1900 at the annual meeting of The National Baptist Convention in Virginia, Burroughs gave a speech "How the Sisters Are Hindered from Helping." This oration gained her national recognition and served as a lightning rod for the formation of the largest Black women's organization in the United States and auxiliary of The National Baptist Convention, known as The Woman's Convention.

Black Baptist women established an unyielding arena for addressing their own concerns. As leaders and faithful followers of the church, the women's Sunday freedoms allowed social developments. For example, wearing hats for occasions and morning worship for them as a people also aided in the development of the Black community with the church as its foundation.

Sunday morning celebrations were the best collections of hymns, up-to-date fashions and ostentatious hats, which were a vocal and visual representation of African American women's styles and socio-economic status. The Sunday morning worship has been important to the community of Black women and their struggle for cultural identity. Furthermore, a big part of that here again was wearing a hat that stood out amongst others in their congregations.

There is so much that can be said as far as the tradition of hat wearing is concerned and how it played a role in the life of the Black church, as well as in the identification of a Black woman who attended Sunday services with a hat on her head, which it was very rare that she would attend hatless. An in-depth study of how Black women co-relate in hats and finery was conducted by Dr. Barbara Rhodes of State University of New York Institute of Technology. Her subject matter was based upon two books, *Living In, Living Out* by Elizabeth Clark-Lewis and *We Too Shall Wear a Crown* by Christopher Davis, who stated that there are plans underway to develop a national service organization comprised of African-American females who are avid hat wearers, entrepreneurs, and who love the arts. Such an organization is designed to empower black men and boys into the fold of entrepreneurship based upon their artistic abilities. Another study was conducted by students from Middleburg College in Middleburg, Vermont, again using *We Too Shall Wear A Crown* by Christopher Davis.

There have been several articles written by various journalists as they seek to report stories on the said tradition as ladies in communities celebrate and work to preserve this rich tradition and the strong legacies left by such women, as the black women who have preceded them in head covering. For example, you will find one written by Nicole Kidder, updated September 29, 2017. A deeply-rooted tradition in the African American community, wearing flamboyant hats to church has both spiritual and cultural significance. The centuries-old custom continues to flourish throughout the Southern U.S. and in strong black Northern communities, including Philadelphia, Chicago, Detroit and Harlem. The dress hats, which are beautifully fabricated and extravagantly decorated, have evolved into an art form and an important cultural symbol.

Prior to the 20th century, most American Christian women commonly followed Corinthians 1:11 and covered their heads in worship. For early African Americans, God's house was not only a sanctuary of hope and salvation in a brutal world, but it was also one of the few places where they were allowed to hold important positions of leadership. Sunday was thus a day of worship and celebration. African American women traded in their drab aprons and knotted head wraps for brightly colored dresses and straw hats gaily decorated with fresh flowers, ribbons and feathers. These heaven-reaching hats were designed to "catch God's eye" in hopes He would hear their prayers.

Elaborately adorned headdresses hold enormous significance in African rituals. American slaves continued the custom of weaving geometric designs, attaching feathers and adding beaded jewelry to straw and fiber hats before attending church. In addition to instilling pride and confidence, the hats remind the wearers to carry themselves like queens. Culturally, church hats became a strong symbol of the ability to triumph over hardships. Worn with the head held high, African American women strut with "Hattitude" while sporting these crowns.

As African Americans gained greater freedoms, the crown evolved into an important status symbol. During the Harlem Renaissance in the 1920s, the growing middle class celebrated their economic successes by purchasing flashy hats and wearing them everywhere, from the office to the speakeasy. Black women appeared in church flaunting colorful, wide-brimmed hats lined in silk, sparkling with rhinestones and trimmed with flower garlands, sassy feathers and delicate lace. Noted African American milliners, which include Grace Bustill Douglass, Mildred Blount and Mae Reeves, achieved fame for their designs as early as the 1800s.

Young girls who dreamed of wearing beautiful hats like their mothers and grandmothers rebelliously rejected the crown as a symbol of oppression and the black bourgeoisie in the 1960s. Still, ridiculed elders kept the tradition alive. In the 1990s, these young women vigorously reembraced the custom as they became the church elders. Although most prominent milliners are now well past retirement age, custom-made designs cost between $100 to $1,000. While many church-going African American women own at least one formal hat, it is not uncommon for devout crown wearers to have one that flawlessly matches each carefully tailored church dress. Shopping for the perfect hat to wear on Easter, Mother's Day and Christmas can take hours.

In writing and photographing their book, *Crowns*, Michael Cunningham and Craig Marberry discovered that numerous unwritten rules for wearing church hats have developed in the African American community. This hat etiquette includes not wearing anything that is wider than the shoulders or darker than the color of the shoe,s and never borrowing or touching someone else's hat, although treasured pieces are often passed on to daughters and granddaughters. While the hat should be the focal point, it must not compete with the matching outfit, jewelry or accessories, such as handbags and gloves.

According to the *Philadelphia Tribune*, one of America's most famous milliners, or hat makers, is remembered in a new permanent collection by the Smithsonian National Museum of African American Culture. The work of Mae Reeves, a milliner to the elite black women of the past, will have her shop re-created in the museum. During the 1940's and 50's, Mae Reeves supplied original hat creations to **Lena Horne, Ella Fitzgerald, Eartha Kitt** and **Marian Anderson**. Reeves was 99 years old at the time of this article, and her granddaughter, Donna Limerick, carries on the memory of her grandmother's legacy by putting Reeve's hats on display. Women such as **Vanilla Beane**, age 94 and another East Coast milliner, kept her shop doors open for decades, **Bené Millinery** on Third Street NW. One of her most famous clients was the late **Dr. Dorothy Height**.

In an article written by Bobbi Booker (*Tribune* Staff Writer), Famed milliner Mae Reeves (seated in a photo not used in this publication) is flanked by celebrity models wearing her hats, from left, Lisa Thomas Laury, ABC 6; Carol Erickson, CBS 3l; Sheinelle Jones and Sue Serio, Fox 29 and Abdul R. Sulayman/*Tribune* Chief Photographer Reeves was present at the "Hats Off to Mae Day" reception that included dozens of family members, friends and admirers of one of Philadelphia's most successful business owners creating extraordinary hats for the new museum, the Smithsonian's 19th and only national museum devoted exclusively to the documentation of African–American life, art, history and culture.

It was expected to open in 2015. "We have an incredible collection that helps us tell Mae's story with her incredible hats," said NMAAHC curator Dr. Renee Anderson. "My minister said I'm not supposed to cuss, so I drooled, I giggled, I danced and I cried. It brings tears to my eyes to think of this incredible woman. The collections speak to the entrepreneurial spirit and tenacity of African Americans through the combining of creativity and business acumen. The ability to take an idea and develop it and come up with a strategy to change the idea from a cerebral concept to a plan that has a measurable outcome and support the concepts of being a productive member of society. Brand loyalty for over 50 years speaks to the loads of networking and outreach in a limiting world." As women's fashion changed in the late 20th century, Reeves' business declined, yet she continued to keep her 60th Street shop open for her "special clients" up until 1997, when she was 85 years old.

"There is nothing easy about a black woman becoming an entrepreneur in the 1940s," said AAMP President Ramona Briscoe Benson. "The fact that this wonderful woman was able to go to the Chicago School of Millinery, come up to Philadelphia and open a business that she was able to maintain, moving from South Philadelphia and serving such women of high regard is something tremendous, and something we need to be proud of her [in] Philadelphia and always keep in mind. Every time we have the opportunity to touch a trailblazer it is special. This woman kept her business open for special clients until she was 85 years old. That happens when you love what you do and you have a passion for your work and art. To be able to keep a business open for that period of time shows us how important those people felt their work to be."

City Representative Melanie Johnson reminded guests how much these elegant hats lifted women's self-esteem and presented Reeves with a ceremonial Liberty Bell. A fashion show highlighting Reeves' vintage designs featured hats worn by several on-air personalities from local television stations who delegated in wearing the head-turning fashion statements

There was a similar observation offered by a professor of history at the University of Alabama in Huntsville, as mentioned by Elizabeth Clark-Lewis. Blacks rarely got to dress up during the work week, so Sunday was primarily the only time they were able to do so. Without regards to the name of the church or the denomination they belonged, it was customary for a Black woman to wear a hat to service.

From African American ladies landing in the Jamestown Colony of Virginia in 1619 with a rag tied around their heads, to the present wearing beautiful, lavish, flamboyant hats for worship and occasions, while it appears as such, hat wearing really is not among a dying breed. While we also think about in this decade, hat wearing is almost like puberty, young ladies feel like they have to wait until they are a certain age in order to begin wearing hats to worship and for occasions. Although there is no time that has been determined for a female to begin this phase of life, a number of them begin by playing dress up, patterning after seeing their mother in her Sunday best, and they view themselves through the mirror. After having done it so many times, it becomes a part of who they are.

The first Sunday in the month has traditionally been when women dress in all white for communion Sunday, or the traditional serving of the Lord's Supper. You can find in almost every Missionary Baptist Church, a deaconess ministry and a senior missionary ministry. On the first Sunday, they are adorned in all white accessories to include an astonishing hat. In the African Methodist Episcopal Church, stewardess members wear white cloth-like head coverings, and in some instances, they provide one for every female who partakes in the supper, just for the sake of having her head covered. In the Apostolic and Pentecostal churches alike, you can find the mother's board dressed in white on almost any given Sunday. I mean, you will see all types of white hats, turbans and tams standing out above those pearly white teeth. You will literally get transfixed on these white hats, after spending so much time in awe.

This book is comprised of historic perspectives of black women who wear hats to church. A part of a series of "Educating Black Boys through the Art of Storytelling," as we have been told on numerous occasions, hats talk. However, you should use the power of your imagination as we walk through this exhibit and portrait showcase. It will give you a greater insight as to the artistic side of how art can tell a story. This exhibit will leave a lingering gleam of consciousness that from time to time will flash across your mind like a gleam of light. The handiwork (Artistic Design) in the hat is so unique that it proves the hypothesis that no one artist sees the same thing, so no matter how many times you may have seen a hat duplicated, it is still the work of one designer. This is all about storytelling, from the artist who creates the design, to the lady who wears the hat. Every detail is just so significant, and they hold true to the historic landmarks of life and events that have taken place in time. Stories are what we read and interpret, told from something as simple as a hat.

This segways into viewing and absorbing how beautiful the universe is as we meditate and think about how significant the lives of these women are to the obstacles they have encountered, and how they found solace in the tradition of wearing hats to church and for occasions, while they have projected beauty outwardly, birthed inwardly. These women have maintained such levels of providence aligned with beauty that even the eye of your heart can bear witness. These hats are like ornaments of our universe, the works of human beings, allowing us to view and recognize these elements as they share stories that will have lasting impacts. Find here what will almost be like the work of an artist who uses lines, shapes and colors, to exemplify tradition and culture to be viewed simply as art. Here you have creativity, originality, and skill, manipulating what can be seen as the characters of letters and numbers. The end results will produce an arrangement of designs and a prolific repertoire of unpredictable nonobjective versions of pure dialogue.

Okay finally, let's take a walk through this cultural exhibit. This I do believe, that the culture of Black women wearing hats to church and for occasions is permanently and indestructibly imbedded in their DNA. This is an honorarium to Black women who have continued to honor the tradition of wearing hats to church. These women not only make wearing hats special, but they have helped to make the image of the Black woman in a hat an allegory for Black Christianity. The Black women who wear hats to church have become a billboard that asserts that "I am somebody and I have given rise to somebody endowed with inalienable rights ever since the beginning of man. (In the words of Dr. Walter James)

When Dr. Walter James sat in orientation for his new teaching job in the New York City School System, he found his superintendent to be wearing an astonishing white hat, and she was clad with white gloves. As Dr. James sat transfixed with his eyes on her hat, he envisioned the hat moving to the rhythm of the words she spoke. As she spoke, it danced to the cadence of her voice and gave conviction to her words and her message. The hat, too, spoke of tasteful personal style, a wholesome upbringing and feminine ascendancy.

Her well-coordinated accoutrements conveyed one theme having four implications; governing or controlling, influence, domination and supremacy. Together they heralded; "I am Black, I am a woman, I am Zinianthropus, the proclaimed and acclaimed mother of humankind who gave birth to civilization in the rift valley under the shadow of Kilimanjaro's Kibo in Eastern Africa. I am Sheba; I am Zipporael; I am Semiramis; I am Amina; I am Candace; I am Cleopatra; I am Dahia-Al-Kahina; I am Hatsheput; I am Nandi; I am Nefertal; I am Nehanda; I am Nzingha; I am Tiye; I am Yaa Asantewa; I am every Black woman who has tread upon the soil of the United States since the first ship alighted in 1619, through the darkness of slavery, through the tedious second half of the 19th century and the fickle of the 20th century. I am the Black woman in the 21st Century who still stands strong and proud; proud of the black women who laid the foundation on which my people stand. I am proud of those who will continue to fortify the base and improve the structure of my nation." (The Late Dr. Walter L. James)

The words of a few of those who have done just that, fortified the base and have improved the structure of the nation of the "Apostles of Her Culture." Below is what a few of them have said when interviewed regarding their historic perspectives.

"As a young girl growing up, my mother and grandmother introduced me to the hat-wearing era.

Of course, the Easter season would be my debut. I was raised being taught that it was proper for a woman to cover her head for morning worship with a hat out of respect. Of course, the gloves were a part of the ensemble. I probably own some one hundred fifty hats. I can always count on my husband to tell me how lovely I look when I'm wearing any one of them, even if it's outlandish. I wear hats on a daily basis, even when I'm working in my yard. I hope that the legacy of Black women wearing hats to church and for special occasions will continue, while I will continue the tradition of wearing them myself. If even I am honored among countless Black women who wear hats to church, I will simply feel like a queen with multiple crowns."

"I remember my first hat when I was a girl not yet twelve. It was Easter and my mother made a red and white dress with a white duster to wear with it. My hat was of white straw with a red ribbon around the crown and streaming down the back. From that time on, hats have been an important part of my wardrobe. To this day, I am complemented very often on the hats I wear. Of the many gifts received, hats have been at the top of list, accompanied by numerous comments such as 'I thought this hat looked like you or I thought you would look nice in this hat.' I feel if it gives you joy to simply receive hats. Even more joy should be exemplified while wearing them. I've often wondered if the love for hats is in the genes or is it something taught, because as much as I like to wear my mother's hats, my three-year-old granddaughter likes to wear them also. "

"I am a retired dietician of District Three Schools, Florence, SC after serving for 35 years, pleasing the children of Lake City, Scranton and Atlantic schools. Hats to me dignify elegance. When I wear hats, they make me feel complete as well compliment my outfit. In addition to the above, hats also function as a warming piece to the head."

"Keeping the tradition of hat-wearing alive is an important role in my life, since my grandmother, in the person of the late Mrs. Rose Ann Johnson, planted the seed. There was something about her when she wore a hat. It thrilled me to see her in one, and as she continued to wear them, it was like I was a tree planted awaiting her to continue to water and nourish, until it was fully grown. Here you have it. I'm fully grown and it thrills me to know that I am wearing a hat to church, just as it did when I saw Grandma with one. "

"A ninety-five-year-old native Newberrian who has lived in Newberry County all of my life, I've had the distinguished honor of being the mother of Newberry County (this honor pertains to all Newberry County female residents) in the year 2004. I've also held the honor of being the mother of her church. I have worn hats to church for Sunday morning worship service all of my life. There is no such thing as a hat-wearing era as far as I am concerned. I do think it is important for a woman to do what the Bible tells her to do and one of those things is to adorn herself by covering her head for Sunday morning worship service. Some of the funnier experiences I have had while wearing my hats come from some of the descriptions the little children at church, as they tried to describe the way the hat looked to them. They usually compared a wide brim of the hat to the wings of an airplane. Over the years, the men still say about the same thing. "That is a pretty hat" or "I like that hat" or they would tell me about somebody they knew who had a hat just like my hat. It is always nice and polite for them to take the time to give me a compliment. I make sure I keep what I call an all occasion hat in my closets. Other than that, I give my hats to other ladies who honor the tradition of always wearing a hat to church. I probably have twenty to twenty-five hats. The ladies need to start wearing hats to church at a young age. Teaching them while they are young will help them to understand why their mothers and grandmothers would not go to church during Sunday morning worship service without wearing a hat. They would put more pride in praising the Lord with their heads. I grew up wearing hats as a young lady and I really enjoyed wearing them, they are very cumbersome when it comes to traveling."

"The women in my church wore hats every Sunday and continue to do so. I was not so aware that the tradition was still prevailing until I went to a funeral and had to purchase one before attending the service so I would be covered. The season of the year is very significant to the hat I wear to Sunday morning worship service. That is why I referred to it as my 'basic stock.'"

"Hats have always been an asset to my attire. I love to wear hats; they coincide with my personality. When I arrive, I don't have to worry. I just remain my kind, soft-spoken self, and I allow my hat to do the rest. When my hat has completed its task, I begin to think, wow, that was like seeing golden apples falling from silver trees."

"I have admired hats since I was a child. It reminds me of when we played dress up. Out of everything I put on, my hat was the most important part. I never felt completely dressed until I had my hat on, and that applies to me even today. When I get dressed for church, my hat is what I consider first. It just adds so much class to any outfit, but most of all it makes me feel like the classy woman that I am. While it embraces my inner beauty, it enhances my outer beauty."

"When I was a little girl, I loved seeing my Grandma Fredrina dress up in her Sunday best. Even though she added her purse and gloves, she said her outfit was not truly complete until she had on her Sunday hat. I remember our walks to church in the summer, me imitating her gait and looking up at her big straw church hat thinking of how one day I'd be just like her and wear an elegant hat on my head. All of the women, momma, aunts, older cousin, and ladies from the community, all had hats placed "just-so" on their heads. I can still visualize the sea of colors and textures waving in agreement with the pastor's stirring message. The church sisters did not even say "Amen;" their hats did the talking for them. As I grew older and began to buy my own hats and soon collected a nice array of styles and colors, I kept my vision of Grandma Fredrina, but also took to the Biblical notion of covering a woman's head in church. To this day, I still don't feel properly dressed for church until I place a sharp hat on my head to compliment my attire. I've passed my love of hats to my daughter and pray I get the opportunity to take my granddaughters to get their first church hat."

"After having watched mother for many years wearing many hats, I began to feel that each person wears a hat that speaks to their own personality. As you will see me with the big brim hat, I have an outgoing happy personality. There is an old saying that you are not fully dressed unless you have your hat on, so today I guess I am fully dressed."

"My earliest memory of wearing a hat goes back to my early childhood, when I was learning how to dress myself. Whenever we left home, we had to have our heads covered. The female is not fully dressed until she is wearing her hat. Wearing the hat during Sunday morning worship service is especially important because Sunday is the Sabbath and we are to keep it HOLY. We are to give God our best, and that includes wearing our best hat to go along with our best outfit and the best of everything else we can give to our father and share with our Christian family. I'm reminded of a black history month program in which the adult education committee's goal was to teach our youth facts about our history. The adults dressed in fashions worn years ago. I dressed in a casual style, comfortable for doing everyday chores. It was a long dress with a ruffled, pleated-hem and apron. My long pig-tail hairstyle with bangs required me to wear a wig and bonnet with a tie under the chin. The shoes were ankle-high brogans. In that outfit, several of the members young and old did not recognize me. I had a lot of fun as they looked for Ms. Frierson (LOL). Usually I get "Who is that young lady in that beautiful hat?" They think I am much younger than I am. At the time of this event, I was 94 years old. I have always owned a hat and I have always shared my hats. I started giving away hats in my early adulthood. I like hats, and those who know me understand that fact about me. Therefore, I usually receive at least one hat on gift-giving occasions, three of four years times a year. If I kept none of the hats I have bought and just a few of the hats I have received at 95 years old, I still would not have enough space for my hat collection. I give away hats all the time and don't keep up with how many I have. I don't think getting younger ladies to wear hats to church is hard to do. We need to practice what we preach by wearing hats to church ourselves and letting the young ladies know we expect them to follow the examples we set. The hats I wear to Sunday morning worship service relate to theme focused during a particular worship service and/or the specific service I am rendering during that service (i.e. singing on the senior choir, etc.)"

"Tradition is defined as the handing down of beliefs, opinions, customs, stories, and more from parents to children. Getting up on Sunday morning, getting dressed, and going to church to serve the Lord was one tradition in our mother's house. Regardless of what happened during the week or on Saturday, we went to church on Sunday. My parents implanted this into all of us, and we continued with our children. Mother believed that if one could go to work, school, and enjoy after school activities, then one could get up and go to church. You must always thank God for your blessings and never forget what He brought you through. I've instilled in my children the idea of being your best at all times. This was true for church and everyday life. When you present yourself before God or man, there should be an excellence in all things including your dress. This idea leads to the tradition of wearing hats to church. Mother believed, and so do I, that if your head and feet were neat and looked right, then you could put on just anything and be dressed up. As children, we watched Mother dress every Sunday morning for church and top off her attire with a matching hat. She watched her mother do the same thing on Sunday mornings. When she was a child, a lady was not dressed if she did not have a hat on. All of my sisters were hat-wearing ladies, and to this day my daughters continue to honor the legacy and tradition of wearing hats to church and for occasions."

"I recall my affiliation with the hat-wearing era came as early as my childhood. My mother used to purchase hats to compliment her outfits. I probably own some one hundred hats or more. I feel it is important for a woman to adorn her head with a hat for morning worship because it sets a more appropriate atmosphere for worship. Hat wearing has been a tradition that has been handed down for generations among the women in my family and is still being practiced. For whatever reason, I always get the feeling of being set apart when I'm wearing a hat. Hats are very attractive depending upon how the milliner designs it, and they are noteworthy of conversation after any affair that would require or simply allow the opportunity for a hat to be worn. Special designs can be created by a milliner who knows your personal style. I typically like a unique hat, huge in size and accented with rhinestones. I am always so amazed at the number of people who want to get up close and personal with my hats, as they desire to feel the fabric and so forth, and a number of them even request to take photographs of it."

"The question has been asked that if hats could talk, what they would say about me? If my hats could talk, they would reveal certain aspects of my attitude, character and lifestyle. I wear hats to give off a regal but yet elegant appeal as they are accessorized with my garments. This is certainly a fashion statement like no other, even if it's no more than dressing down for occasions."

"My spouse (a deceased pastor) used to adore me in hats. He has stated on occasions that wearing a hat adds a touch of class and elegance to an outfit. We both wore hats on many occasions. My son usually asks the question, "Oh Mom, where did you get that hat from, or he may simply say, "That is really pretty." I truly believe that the tradition of hat-wearing and covering the head for worship should remain, although I will do my part in keeping it alive. Never do I feel like I'm not passing on the tradition, simply because I am constantly working on passing it down via my family, constantly purchasing new hats, and encouraging others to accessorize them with their ensembles. I stand tall on the battlegrounds of saving such a rich and beautiful tradition, working to bring others into the fold of wearing hats to church and for occasions. It's always an amazing experience to see how different any female looks during and after wearing a hat for the first time."

"If I were selected among countless Black women who wear hats to church to be honored in a formal celebration, I would be honored and extremely proud. I have been a participant in many hat or fashion shows over the years because people are aware that I love to wear elegant hats, and of course they have to be unique and different."

"I recall becoming affiliated with wearing hats through my mother, who was an avid hat-wearer. I probably own well over seventy hats. Wearing a hat is an important part of worship, as it has been in our communities for years. Knowing that you have a stunning hat on during Sunday morning worship makes you feel really good about yourself. My husband would say to me after a glimpse of the final touch (my hat), "You buy too many hats." I like to often think, if my hats could talk, what would they say? If they could, they would say that I am a lover of God, love morning worship, but most of all love the opportunity to showcase a fabulous hat. Hat-wearing is such a rich tradition and I feel like it should be passed on to the next generation of ladies, in order that they may keep the torch lit."

"Every hat is beautiful in its own way. My mother Mary Alice Turner always admired hats but she always thought she was too tall to wear them. When I was a little girl growing up in Boardman, North Carolina, I often stayed with my grandmother Alice Floyd Turner. She was indeed a hat lady. It seems as though all the women at First Born Holiness Church wore hats, to include the young and the seasoned. Most of the hats were very unique. I seriously doubt that I will ever see those kinds of hats again. I have always admired their different styles and colors, some were tall, some were wide and some I just couldn't figure out."

"I started wearing hats at the age of seven. My grandmother said I had to keep a hat on my head or I could catch a cold, which meant having to take castor oil. So, of course I chose the hat. Back in 1968, money was not easy to come by so Grandma made the majority of my hats and hers. I can remember one special hat that reminded me of a rainbow because it had so many beautiful colors. It was my favorite because I could wear it with anything. If that hat could sing, it would sing a song that says, "Every hat is beautiful in its own way; we will never vanish for we are here to stay.""

"My husband Tommy is my biggest supporter. He buys all of my hats today. He always says he wants his wife to look good. I will continue until I leave to receive my seat on one of heavens mourner's benches."

"Hats have always been interesting to me. I have enjoyed seeing the various styles, and wearing them as well. Growing up in the South may have had some impact on me. My mother wore them to church almost every Sunday. I wore them as a teen, which really added to the intrigue. I began noticing hats again when I became affiliated with the Greater Highway Churches of Christ Inc., under the dynamic leadership of the Bishop R.F. Davis."

"I think that each hat is unique and the wearer should feel special. I personally think that hats are not for everyone. I feel partial to the larger hats, and at one point, I would only wear a certain style of hat. As I matured in age, various other styles began to appeal to me. Hats accentuate ones' attire and add a little more flare, and drama, depending on how much noise that hat makes. I was inspired as a child and plan to continue throughout life. I have already begun stacking hats into my husband's walk-in closet. He does not mind anyway because if he did, he would not continue to buy them for me."

"At the young age of fourteen, my father began purchasing hats from Julius Garfield to make me feel special. I love wearing hats. Those hats have made me the indignant Black woman that I am today, proud, full of life, and more precious than jewels."

"I love the hats because of a great desire to have my attire complimented. I wear them in the winter to keep my head warm and in summer to protect me from the sun. I wear hats because they make sense."

"Growing up in rural Maxton, N.C. and going to church on Sunday morning, my parents instilled the impression that one should not attend service without her hat. Both my parents wore hats to church. I feel that a lady is not fully dressed until she has a hat on. Many of the ladies say that hats do not become them or it doesn't fit their face or their head, but I always seem to be able to convince them that there is a hat for every head and face. My motto is, the letter (i) is not a (i) without the dot on top of it, so a lady's attire is not complete until she has a hat on her head."

"I recall as though it was yesterday how my great grandmother, grandmother, my mother had and a host of relatives and friends were always adorned with gloves, handbags, and handkerchiefs as they made their way to worship, but among all of these things the one thing that stood out the most would be their hats. I feel that it is important that a woman adorn her head with a hat for morning worship because it adds to the serenity of the service. Whenever you put on the sophisticated look, your entire demeanor is different. Ask me how I know? I own well over one hundred hats, and if they could talk they would just look at me and smile. They'd say, "You go, girl," which is what I always say each morning after I place my hat on my pretty grey hair. People were so accustomed to seeing me wearing a hat until once I was presiding over a missionary society meeting, where-in I did not wear a hat because I'd just come in from the heat outside and decided to take my hat off for a moment. Strangely none of the members entered the room. It was said that another lady was hosting a meeting in that room simply because my hair was showing and not my hat. My husband always made sure I have the right hat and it was coordinated properly as far as color with the suit or dress I was wearing. My son is always bragging to his peers, as he does on a constant basis, about the number of hats I own. My daughter buys hats for me all the time and I get them as gifts from the parishioners, from my church and friends in the community. I don't think this tradition will ever fade, as I reflect upon photos from the 60's and 70's. I noticed that persons wore hats even though they had an abundance of hair. I will continue to wear hats to church and for occasions, and continue to share hats with persons who are less fortunate but still have a desire to look good."

"Hats are so precious to me, and I love the idea of knowing that I am fully dressed, when I have my hat on."

"I admire hats because they make me feel complete and assure me that for either church or an occasion, my attire is complete. I am comfortable wearing them. I like soft-spoken hats, being a soft-spoken person, I don't have to make a great deal of noise when I arrive on the grounds of the Pleasant Grove Missionary Baptist Church Ministries. They just know I'm present because of the still, soft-spoken hat that adorns my head."

"'If it had not been for the Lord who was on my side, now may Israel say…' Psalms 124:1. I was taught as a young girl to be meek and always have good manners so as I select my hats for Sunday morning worship, I think of calm attire and accessories, something that I will just serve as an appetizer, because after they get one look at my hat, if there was room for hunger from the appetizer, trust me they would be full."

"When I think on hats, I think on the one thing that means so much to me, the one thing that helps to make my personality, the one thing that makes me stand out in a positive way, and that one thing is a hat. I normally walk to morning service because I live behind my church, and on any given Sunday you will know it is me because of my strut. Yes, I can strut because I know my attire is complete, from my shoes, my suit, just everything, because I have on a hat, and not just any ordinary hat, a custom-designed hat, whether it be by Christopher Davis or any other designer, you will know T is present, and she is not taking any prisoners. What you see is what you get, and make no mistake about it, they often call me 'Ms. Bethlehem Missionary Baptist Church,' because I serve them raw fashions and fabulous hats."

"I will bless the Lord at all times; His praise shall continually be in my mouth. When I rise on Sunday morning, doubt has no place in my mind. I get up feeling no ways tired. I rise to tell the saints that He still lives, He still delivers, and He is working miracles. As I rise though, I kind of feel what my attire for the day will be like, so first I select my hat. It is amazing though that although it is not a religious practice that I must adorn my head with a hat. But as a female in the ministry, 'modest apparel' means to be complete. So, do not enter the sacred place without your hat on. As we are called to serve, we should remember what finer womanhood really means, and with our hats on our peers will know what it looks like."

"I'm a keeper of the tradition of wearing hats to church and for occasions. I have more than one hundred hats in my wardrobe. No room in my house escapes being adorned by hats of all colors, all sizes and shapes. My love for hats has affectionately earned my nickname as the "Hat Lady." I have hats from New York, Germany, Paris and of course numerous designed by Christopher Davis. When I put on a hat, I feel totally dressed and complete."

"Here you have a true southern lady who feels I'm not properly dressed without a hat to adorn my head. I've admired and worn hats since I was a young girl. My first hat was a black one, which was too old for a girl who was just sixteen, but who cared. I just wanted to wear a hat. It belonged to my mother. My love for hats extends further than the church walls. Some may view me as a southern lady as I tend to my flowers in a big floppy straw hat or stroll the streets in a casual brim. Of all the hats that adorn my head, none can compare to my glow that radiates through me when I put on my pure white, starched nurse's hat that says 'LPN.' This is the pride of all of my hats. I'm often thought of as a lady of distinction who knows where, how and when to wear, a brim, a bonnet, and even a HAT."

"Hats are not a strange thing to me. I have worn hats as a child, and they were part of my uniform during my early years of schooling. Presently, I wear hats for various occasions, and hardly ever will you see me serve a family during a funeral service without a hat on. Hats tend to make any female in the funeral industry look the part. They offer a professional appearance, give off dignified vibes to those who are among you while providing a service. I have hats of all colors, sizes, shapes, and forms, you name it. My husband often wonders what is going to become of these hats when I take off my immortal hat and exchange it for my mortal crown. With that said, perhaps they could just open a museum. I became affiliated with hat-wearing from almost the age of one, because my mother never took me out without something on my head. As I grew older and entered the early teen years of my life, I can recall my parents enrolling me into Palmer Memorial Institute, located in North Carolina, under the direction of Dr. Charlotte Hawkins-Brown. I entered my ninth-grade year, and of course wearing hats and gloves were a part of our uniform attire. We wore hats and gloves to class, outings downtown, and of course to church. We, of course, had to ensure that we wore pantyhose and heels. After becoming a mortician, it was just embedded in me that it was appropriate to wear a hat as you honor the life of the deceased and serve the family of the deceased in a professional manner. I am not exactly sure how wearing a hat on a funeral came to be, but like many other funeral service organizations, I do not attend a funeral hatless, and I do not allow the female attendants on my staff to work a funeral hatless. I can't say exactly how many hats I own, but I own quite a few of many colors, sizes, shapes, looks, jazzed up, simple, plain, etc. I have hats designed by tons of designers, but I have purchased many from Christopher Davis, a designer that I know personally. He, my grandson and my granddaughter all agree that my hats exceed three hundred, but they stop there so that it doesn't appear as though I am being boastful. I am simply one lady who loves hats and enjoys wearing them. I rarely loan my hats to people. There have been occasions when I have worked funerals and people have asked me for a hat, and I honored their request and gave it to them. I have even gone as far as to assist staff members with getting started with their hat collection. I can recall once an old friend who had moved away came back home to bury her mother, and of course with having to travel and having so many things on her mind, she forgot to bring hats. When she reminded me that she left her hat and needed one, of course I allowed her to use one that was especially dear to me. This one was designed by Christopher Davis, but it was especially precious. I allowed her to use it to honor her mother's life and legacy. I think it is so fitting for a lady to wear hats to church on Sunday morning; it just makes her so complete, especially when she has coordinated it with a matching bag, suit, gloves and heels. If my hats could talk, they would say that I look really sophisticated and grand in my church go-to-meeting finery. My husband thinks I look nice, and he approves of my look when I am completely dressed. But he also says that if he had in cash right now, the amount of money I have spent over the years in all of the hats that I own, and or have given away, he would not be so broke (LOL). My daughters and granddaughters are all lovers of hats, but they would rather see me in one first. This gives them an idea of the look they need to have for a particular occasion. They are futuristic, hat-wearing ladies indeed."

"I feel complete and fully dressed when I have a hat on. I love the way Chris makes his hats. He makes them just like they are made especially for me and they fit right to the T. I always get great comments about my hats. When I'm among the saints at Palmetto Deliverance Ministries, they constantly inquire about where I purchase my hats and or who the designer is."

"I have always admired hats. I feel that I'm not completely dressed without a hat on, especially during morning service. Hats embrace my self-esteem. I never try to attend service hatless. There are numerous women who attend St. John African Methodist Episcopal Church who wear beautiful hats. The hat-wearing was so intriguing when we were under the leadership of a pastor who would host the hat contest of the day. From the pulpit before dismissal of any given service, he would announce who he thought had the prettiest hat on that day. You must know that the competition was fierce. I normally sit down in the corner adjacent to the gospel choir, and of course several of their members wear hats. I probably own nearly one hundred hats; they occupy space in my living room and many other areas throughout my house. Before Sunday morning comes, I have already decided on dinner, have my chores done, and my hat is finally down for morning service. But rest assured that no matter who wears what type of hat, where they purchased it from, or even how much they paid for it, they are going to have to bring it, because I'll be there waiting with my hat on."

"The tradition of wearing hats was handed down to me through a deceased "adopted mother." After she passed, a lot of her hats were stored that no one wore, so I decided to wear them in her memory. She wore hats to church every Sunday. Hats have always been the symbol of a well-dressed, well-organized, and mature women. As a black woman, I have always felt that it was our tradition. A hat seems to complete the outfit for church. Something seems to be missing without it. A hat brings out the lady in you. I wear hats to accentuate my physical features and complement my attire. I never feel completely dressed until I have my hat on. It adds so much class to any outfit, but most of all, it makes me feel like the classy woman I am. While it embraces my inner beauty, it enhances my outer beauty. Hats signify elegance and when I wear them, they make me feel complete and assure me that my attire is complete as well. One of my funnier moments took place when I went back to my hometown for the 45th reunion of my high school class. I had no idea it was dress-down Sunday, and I popped up dressed to impress, and you know my hat was laid to the side. I mean I was looking good and you can imagine how I felt (LOL). There are times when men pay close attention to my hats, and from time to time they say to me, "Girl, you are really wearing that hat." "You look as though you just stepped out of a magazine." "That hat is wearing you." "Where are you modeling today?" I store my hats all over the house to include walk-in-closets, behind the sofas, etc. I own about 75 hats now. I had a house fire, and of course my collection was destroyed, so I had to start over: Christ is head of the church and I feel more connected to the service if my head is covered under the blood of Jesus. Hats reassure me of the woman I am."

"I started wearing hats to church at a young age. I think every woman should wear hats to church. I love the multiple compliments that I receive on my usually large hats. I always felt though the bigger the better. Over the years, my family has given me hats for every occasion that they felt it to be fitting, and I never changed words, because to me it was more than any dollar amount that could be given. I know that I own over one hundred hats. I have three daughters who have adopted the tradition of wearing hats. My granddaughter wants me to will my hats to her, after I have been called from labor to reward. My hats keep me feeling young and looking beautiful. I have to hold on to this era. I have nineteen grandchildren and twenty-four great grandchildren, so if this is what it takes for me why not? Knowingly everybody in my community calls me the "Hat Lady." When I arrive at Bethel African Methodist Episcopal

Church, I feel like I have stepped on to the red carpet like ones that the celebrities walk down when they arrive at the Oscars. Yes at the Oscars many ladies give up gowns, but when I go to give up a praise to God almighty I give the saints hats, hats and more hats."

"My mother was a hat-wearing woman and I followed in her footsteps. She always said, "a woman isn't properly dressed if she doesn't wear a hat." I started wearing hats to church when I was nineteen years old, and to this date, I own some seventy-five hats. I do not loan my hats nor do I borrow hats from others. I have two sisters and a daughter who wear hats. The same policy is in place with them; they do not loan or borrow hats either. We all have different tastes when it comes to hats, and of course our styles are different. When a time occurred that I could not find a ready-made hat to match an outfit I was preparing to wear, I simply made one myself. When I was younger I loved wearing outlandish, eye-catching hats, but as I have matured, I've become more conservative in selecting what's best for me. In my community, most African-American women dress to impress, especially when going to worship. Of course, hats are an intricate part of our attire. I have every color in the rainbow included in my collection, simply because each hat matches or can be coordinated with any outfit I own. My hats are appropriate for various seasons. I have always taken very good care of my hats and will continue to do so. I wrap and stuff the crowns with tissue paper and store them by color codes in hat boxes. My Fall/Winter hats are usually wrapped in moth-proof bags with cedar chips. Some of the hats I have owned more than forty years, but due to the love and care given unto them, a number of people think they are brand new when I wear them."

"I am I guess a late-bloomer considering I am now sixty-three years young. I was introduced to wearing hats in a real sense by one of my church members. Although I only own about six hats and intend to purchase more, I do feel it is important that a woman adorn her head with a hat for worship. Now of course I was already a sharp dresser and a very attractive female. The hats add a few notches more of sophistication, and that raises the eyebrows of the senior single men in the congregation."

(On The Cover) "Many years ago, my late brother-in-law sent a messenger to my office in New York City to deliver a package to me. He told the messenger to look for the investigator with the "Rag" (Turban) on her head. Needless to say, he found me without a problem. I remember my mother saying that a lady was not dressed unless she was wearing a hat. I have casual and dressy hats, large hats and small hats, pretty hats and unusual hats to say the least. (I don't town an ugly hat.) My sons, nieces and friends never ask what I want for my birthday or Christmas, they know to buy me a hat! If they go away and bring me a souvenir, it is a hat! I have hats in every closet in every room, including the attic. Last count, my hats totaled one hundred plus. Every now and then, I donate hats to my favorite charity. All of my hats are one of a kind with one exception: there was a time that someone was wearing a hat just like mine. You can image where that hat is now! My favorite charity! My hats range in price from fifty cents to two hundred fifty dollars. Recently I went to a hat shop that was going out of business. I picked up a hat and took it to the counter. The clerk said, "That will be fifty cents."

I was sitting in church one Sunday when my eighty-year-old friend touched me on my shoulders and told me that if I ever wore that wide black hat again and sat in front of him, he was going to shoot it off my head! That hat is now reserved for evening funerals when I am sitting in the back of the church. (In the words of the late Mrs. Ethel M. Dewitt-Retired Fraud Investigator New York, New York, Resident of Orangeburg, South Carolina at the time of her transition.

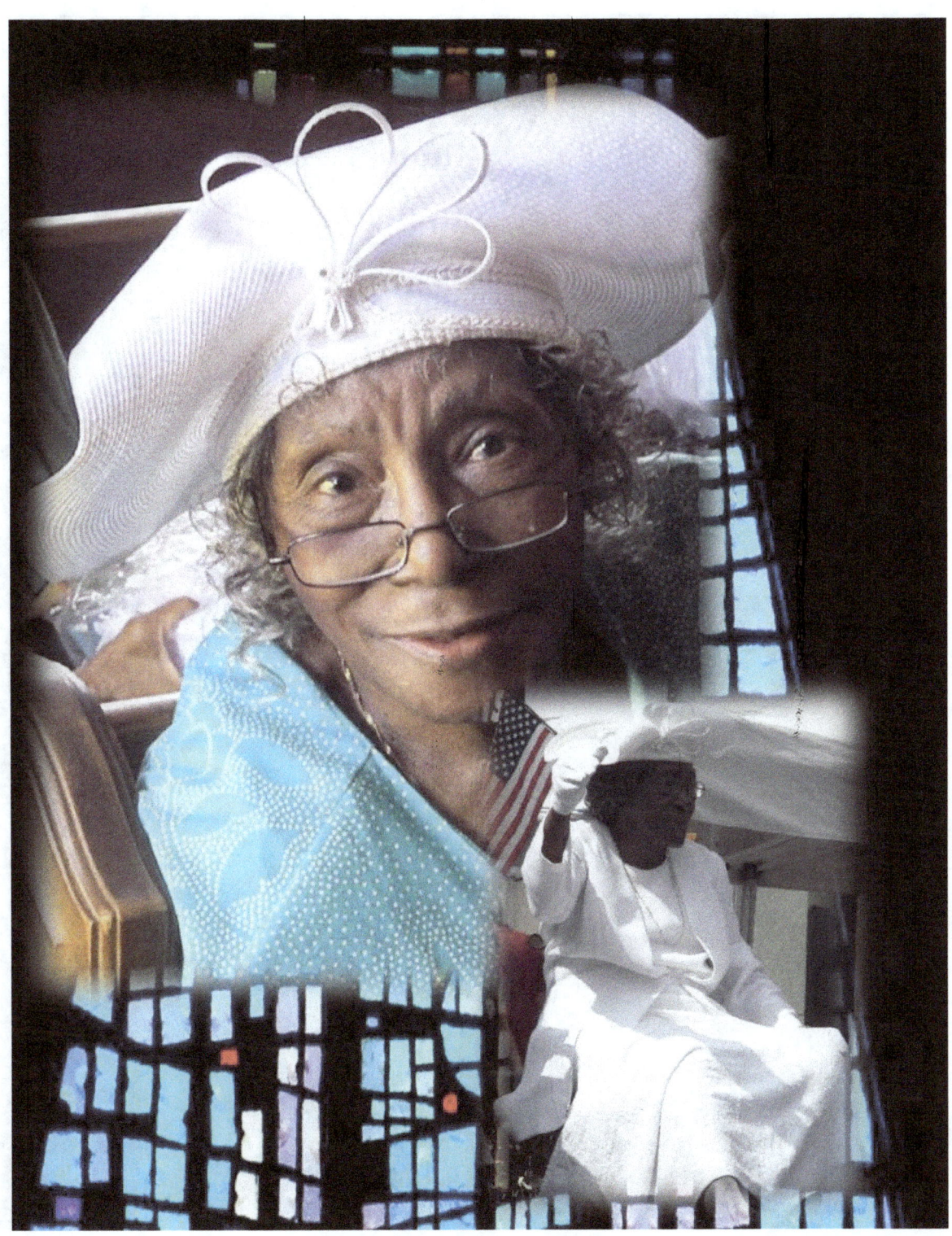

New Life Hat Society, Inc.

Mr. Davis is the Organizer and CEO of the New Life Hat Society Inc., a not for profit organization comprised of African-American females who are entrepreneurs, artists and females whose professions generate a residual income. This organization is designed to empower primarily black boys into entrepreneurship based upon their artistic.

The organization places a great deal of energy on combatting illiteracy as it recognizes and celebrates the knowledge of black boys when they engage in a conversation with others. If these young men can read and comprehend what they read, they can lead. Thus, the organization trains them to fight the phobia of addressing a crowd, while equipping these young people for the world of entrepreneurship.

While some may not understand the significance of black women wearing hats to church and black boys becoming entrepreneurs, it is a prime example of how the paradigm of service equates success. As a service to other young black boys who are artistically inclined, Davis is not only providing platforms but demonstrating how to utilize them in efforts to increase success for those who ultimately desire to be entrepreneurs. "It works because we work it!"

Email: newlifehatsociety@gmail.com

Website: newlifesociety.org

HadassahsCrownPublishing.com

HadassahsCrown@gmail.com

864-708-1214

www.ingramcontent.com/pod-product-compliance
Lightning Source LLC
Chambersburg PA
CBHW082105280426
43661CB00089B/867